Sunday *of* the Living Dead

Sunday of the Living Dead

©1995 by Robert Kirby

All rights reserved

Printed in the United States

Library of Congress Cataloging-in-Publication Data

Kirby, Robert, 1953-

Sunday of the Living Dead / by Robert Kirby.

p.   cm.

ISBN 1-885628-49

1. Church of Jesus Christ of Latter-day Saints–Humor. 2. Mormon Church–Humor.

3. Mormons–Humor. I. Title.

BX8638.K57   1995

289.3'32--dc20   95-40692

CIP

1 2 3 4 5

Cover illustration by Pat Bagley

Design by Richard Erickson and Pat Bagley

Sunday *of* the Living Dead

A COLLECTION OF
MORMON ESSAYS AND
CARTOONS BY THE
SALT LAKE TRIBUNE'S

ROBERT KIRBY

AND

PAT BAGLEY

BUCKAROO BOOKS

In a serious world, good humor provides a vital release. And when we see some, we'll be sure to print it. Until then, we've decided to make do with this collection of columns from the *Salt Lake Tribune's* Robert Kirby, with a few offerings from the *Trib's* cartoonist and social commentator Pat Bagley thrown in for illumination.

Those who have followed Robert Kirby's column know what they are in for in this collection. While he tries to steer clear of Mormon doctrine, when it comes to the sacred cows of our traditions and culture, it's open season. If his gibes hit close to home, it's because too often the world which Kirby lampoons is the one where we live. If his barbs sting, it's with the discomfort that sometimes comes with looking in a mirror or a microscope and seeing ourselves how and where we really are. Even if you don't like Robert Kirby, more often than not you find yourself having to grudgingly agree. After all, if we can't laugh at ourselves and our culture, we leave it for others to do less kindly.

We are printing our new LDS humor titles under the logo of "Angels fly because they take themselves lightly" and hope you will enjoy the books in the spirit with which we produce them, one of light-hearted, thoughtful fun.

—the publishers

This book

is dedicated to

everyone who's

ever fallen asleep

in church.

One of the reasons that Mormons believe so fervently in near-death experiences is because we have one every Sunday. It's called church.

Sitting there on a folding chair, your limbs grow numb, your eyes glaze over, and your thinking becomes sluggish. Only the shrieking of small children prevents you from slipping completely away and becoming a gospel zombie.

Hold on, the gospel of Jesus Christ isn't church. It's certainly a far cry from the Tupperware Third Ward that most of us attend every Sunday. There the purpose seems to be to get people to dwell on the importance of the next life by making them wish they were dead in this one. Sunday School in the Tupperware Third Ward is like a morgue only with day-care.

No, the gospel isn't the problem. It's the instructors who have fallen into the trap of mindlessly scrolling down a list of prepre-pared, simplistic questions until you wonder if they missed being born as fence posts by virtue of a limited cerebral cortex. If Sunday School teachers teach you anything other than how to sleep with your eyes open, it's by accident rather than design.

Which brings us to the purpose (and disclaimer) of this book. Please make a note of it. *Sunday of the Living Dead* is not intended to be a replacement for the official church manuals.

However, if used sparingly, this book can serve as a teaching supplement. You may want to check with your bishop first, though. For the sake of alleviating a little church boredom, there's no point in angering the guy who can give you a job in the ward nursery. You may have been afraid that Sunday School was slowly killing you, but get stuck in the nursery and you'll wish it had.

So, whether *Sunday of the Living Dead* makes you mad or makes you laugh, it will hopefully keep you awake. If it does, that puts us one up on the manual.

Pat & KIRBY

CONTENTS

5 Kinds *of* **M*o*rmons**

I n the entire world, there are only five kinds of Mormons.

LIBERAL MORMONS: This includes all Mormons who attend church only when they feel like it. LMs vote anywhere to the left of the Republican party, are not rabidly pro-life, and don't believe that every word that falls from the lips of a General Authority represents the actual personal opinion of Jesus Christ.

LMs are going to hell. Just ask any of the other four kinds of Mormons. On the other hand, LMs

LIBERAL MORMONS

think the intolerance and naïveté of other Mormons is more of a threat to mankind than Russian missiles, wheat weevils, or R-rated movies.

GENUINE MORMONS: Nearly every Mormon thinks this is the kind of Mormon he represents. In reality, GMs are about as rare as, oh, say, angels or golden plates.

True GMs are unimpressed with themselves and their own opinions. They are affable, easygoing, and keenly interested in the well-being of others. They live various lifestyles, have a variety of friends, and, when compared to the more outlandish lifestyles of other Mormons, tend to be dang near invisible. A friend of

GENUINE MORMONS

mine says this is because all GMs have been translated.

Studies have proven there are only eleven GMs on the face of the earth. Two of them live in Utah, three in the remainder of the United States, two in South America, one each in Japan, Canada, Samoa, and Spain. There are no GMs in California or Idaho. There was a twelfth GM in England, but she died.

CONSERVATIVE MORMONS: These kinds of Mormons are the suit and flowered dress crowd you see at church. They tend to be overweight and Republican. They attend church ninety-five percent of the time but may, if pressed hard enough, admit to sleeping clear through General Conference. They pay tithing on ten percent of their net income and have 4.5 children. The homes of CMs are decorated with Relief Society-produced

CONSERVATIVE MORMONS

knickknacks. CMs humor LMs because God says they have to. Seventy-five percent of the LDS church is CM, and ninety-nine percent of all CMs were born into the Church.

ORTHODOX MORMONS: This kind of Mormon would not miss church for the death of a relative. Left to their own devices, OMs would eventually make the bringing of dry cereal in Tupperware bowls to sacrament meeting a gospel ordinance. OM women stop having children at thirty-five because thirty-six is too many, even for them.

OMs are scared of Russians, MTV, and accidentally partaking of the sacrament with their left hands. They believe LMs are children of the devil.

ORTHODOX MORMONS

OMs pay tithing based on their gross income and believe that Diet Coke is part of the Word of Wisdom.

NAZI MORMONS: 10 percent of the LDS church is NM. Of that 10 percent, 90 percent live in Utah, most within potlucking distance of BYU. NMs claim Diet Coke is the same thing as heroin, and heaven is a multi-level mar-

NAZI MORMONS

keting system of glory.

NMs believe French kissing is cause for excommunication. They routinely take church advice and improve on it: If no single dating until sixteen is good, no single dating until the draft age is even better.

NMs pay tithing based on their gross income plus the stuff they get from the bishop's storehouse.

5 Kinds of non-Mormons

Fair is fair. In the entire world, there are only five kinds of non-Mormons. Basically.

The first kind of non-Mormon is the IGNORANT NON. Ig-nons know utterly zip about Mormons and aren't interested in knowing more, thank you very much. Ig-nons, despite lofty General Conference claims to the contrary, make up about 49/50ths of the earth's entire population. Or, say,

IG-NONS

8.6 billion Ig-nons per each of the five kinds of Mormons. The vast majority of Ig-nons won't ever be home taught and will no doubt spend the rest of eternity caring not a whit less.

TOLERANT NONS make up the next largest group of non-Mormons. From a purely Mormon point of view, Tol-nons are about the best kind of non that Mormons can hope for. Tol-nons think Mormons are quaint but nice and relatively harmless—except during General Conference when conversion sentiments are whipped into a banzai frenzy.

TOL-NONS

Most Tol-nons plan their out-of-state vacations around April and October, both months when Mormons are practically begging to mow and water non lawns and feed non pets.

Tol-nons don't particularly care what Mormons do with them after they're dead so long as Mormons leave them alone while they're alive.

IRKED NON-MORMONS come in next, both in terms of number and the amount of anti-Mormon noise they make.

Like Ig-nons, Irk-nons know relatively zip about Mormons. The difference being that Irk-nons *think* they know everything.

IRK-NONS

In reality, Irk-nons only know that they can't buy sex, place a bet, or have a drive-up abortion in Utah. Irk-nons have a hard time understanding why a state founded by Mormons, populated largely by Mormons, and generally run by Mormons should reflect mostly Mormon values.

This marked inability to grasp simple cause-and-effect may explain the general lack of rocket scientists among Irk-nons.

FURIOUS NON-MORMONS come next. Fur-nons are not interested in live-and-let-live with Mormons. Mormons are wrong, wrong, wrong. If you've got sixty seconds, and even if you don't, Fur-nons will tell you all about Adam/God, poly-gamy, Danites, Mountain

FUR-NONS

Meadows, and tithing diverted to the Contras.

When it comes to Mormonism, Fur-nons are characterized by the same enormous intolerance they routinely accuse Mormons of. The difference being that Fur-nons see their behavior as being insightful and objective.

RABID NON-MORMONS are the next and last. Rab-nons are a distinct minority among non-Mormon types. However, because Mormons as a whole are hypersensitive about persecution, they routinely confuse the other four types of nons with Rab-nons, making Rab-nons seem more prolific.

RAB-NONS

Most Rab-nons can trace their family roots to Missouri, and from there directly to some cave. Rab-nons cry that anything even remotely connected with Mormonism is out-and-out evil. In fact, now that there are so dang many Mormons, they should be taken off the endangered species list and allowed to be hunted with dogs and helicopters.

This non study showed one additional characteristic about nons, namely that ex-Mormons are only rarely found in the Ig-non, Tol-non, and even Irk-non categories. Most ex-Mormons were found in the Fur-non and

Rab-non categories. However, because of diligent missionary efforts by Mormons, Ex-nons are almost evenly scattered through the five kinds of Mormons.

Confessions of a Sunday School junkie

Mondays are bad, aren't they? On Monday mornings, the only possible way to get to the bathroom from your bed is on your belly.

For some people, this is the natural result of a weekend filled with beer bashes and drug parties. However, for Mormons, Mondays are especially bad because we're suffering from the debilitating effects of something much worse.

When you see Mormons staggering into work Monday morning, you know they're hung over from Sunday School.

Having been hooked on Sunday School at an early age by neglectful and abusive parents, I sometimes reflect on what it would be like to be a non-attender. My life might be infinitely more relaxing if all I had to cope with during the weekend were the fear of AIDS, the police, my drug supplies, and a failing liver. I'm not coveting, mind you. Just reflecting.

The average Mormon isn't up to the rigors of Sunday School. Most of us sensed this at a very early age, say about the time our parents started dressing us up like miniature Republicans and dragging us across the parking lot of church. We screamed and fought this inhumanity, sometimes even resorting to flushing our neckties down the toilet. It was all for naught. Eventually, we became hooked ourselves.

The effects of our Sunday School addiction become more pronounced the older we get. Older people don't scream and fight it, but look how many of them pass out in the middle of it. They put on a brave face, though— even if they're snoring.

The insidiousness of Sunday School addiction is evident in the number of you who this very minute are saying, "Well, my gol, what's wrong with Sunday School?" See? You're hooked so bad you don't even know it.

Sunday School itself isn't bad for your mind. Neither is just growing marijuana because it's attractive. It's the THC (Talk your Head into a Coma) in a Sunday School lesson that erodes your consciousness. Look how we just sit mindlessly through rhetorical questions that would insult the intelligence of most turtles.

"Did Lehi love his family?" was the question in Sunday School a few months ago. "Did he really love them?"

Most of the class absently nodded. The rest were unconscious, some drooling. I couldn't take it anymore. I've been trying real hard to kick Sunday School or at least cut way back.

"He hated them!" I burst out. "Will you people wake up! Lehi took his family into the wilderness so they'd die of thirst."

I'm sorry, but the only way to combat the numbing effects of stupid gospel questions is with stupid gospel answers.

Alas, most of the class was too far gone to notice my attempt to kick the habit. A few roused themselves and flipped through their scriptures to see if I was right, but it was hopeless.

The mind-numbing effects of Sunday School filter down through the various levels, reaching even the most vulnerable. Young men and women are subjected to things like, "Should you have sex with leather-clad strangers or love God, hmm?" or "Why is it important today that we not become serial killers?"

In Primary, they push stupid Sunday School questions like, "Bobby, if you don't stop hitting little Willy on the head with a hymnal, I'll have to take you to your parents. Is that what you want?" I mean is that cold or what?

Sometimes you'll see people trying to kick Sunday School—lost souls stumbling into Sunday School rehab centers down at 7-11, or going it cold turkey alone at home in front of the tube. Either way, it's tough.

A Moving experience

I had a spiritual experience Saturday morning. The Spirit said that no matter what I heard in General Conference on Sunday, the Mormon radicals and feminists are right: There's absolutely no reason why men and women can't be total and exact partners in the gospel work.

There, I said it.

My spiritual experience occurred at the exact moment that Dale, Doug, Ray, and I were hoisting a freezer loaded with 2,000 pounds of corn dogs and deer meat through a basement window. The instant before my spine turned into a Slinky, the Spirit revealed to me that I've done this moving bit at least two hundred times too many—and that it's the Relief Society's turn.

That's right, there's nothing in the scriptures that says the Relief Society sisters can't be the ones who go over to a new move-in's house on a Saturday and drag a piano and a washing machine up three flights of stairs.

No reason, either, why the elders quorum can't be in charge of fixing meals for families with new babies or dead kin. In fact, as a Mormon intellectual, this is the sort of gender equality that I demand from my church.

LDS women deserve the right to experience laying some hands on a chest of drawers loaded with bowling balls and concrete and helping the Spirit move it through eight doorways and up a flight of stairs without scratching it. It's fellowshipping in its most pure form.

Speaking as someone who has lugged one piano too many, I think fixing meals for families in need would be a way cool spiritual experience, one that elders and high priests have been denied too long.

Say somebody in the ward has a baby or a kidney stone. The elders quorum president calls you up to take some meals over to them.

"I know you're busy arranging those Fritos and Slim Jims for the taster table next week, Ralph," he says, "so just keep it simple."

Concerned, you rummage through your pantry and hustle straightaway to the home of the afflicted with a sack of malt balls, some jerky, and a sixer of root beer. Hey, if the spirit of the gesture really is more important than the meal itself, you don't even have to show up. Use your Visa card and order in pizza.

The same is not true for moving ward members in and out of their homes. Whoever's assigned this gospel chore has to actually go there and sweat like special stevedores.

As a longtime priesthood holder, I have deep, abiding memories of the gospel in action: long lines of sweating men silhouetted against an evening sun, singing calypso songs as they unload ninety tons of sacked wheat from the musty hull of a U-Haul.

Hey-oh. We got de priesthood,
we got de wheat.
Hey-oh. We work like de donkey,
ain't we neat.

OK, so that's an apostate idea. The truth is, God didn't intend for men and women to be exactly equal in the gospel work. Proof isn't in the Book of Mormon or a back issue of *Sunstone* magazine, either. Proof is inside the Ryder truck parked in front of your new neighbor's house.

If men and women were intended to be equal, the prophets would've told us to store Cheetos instead of wheat. Mormon hymns would be accompanied by flutes and guitars instead of pianos the size of bank vaults. And we wouldn't have family units the size of infantry platoons.

Whoever gets stuck doing it, helping people move into their new home is an important fellowshipping tool. It's the best way to get to know your neighbors. By the time you finish toting their belongings, you'll be intimately familiar with their tax records, what kind of music they like, how doofy they looked on their wedding day, and their preferred method of birth control.

Short of a disciplinary council or a potluck dinner, you can't get closer to someone than that.

Kids + Church = hell

You can always tell when your bishop admires your courage or hates your guts. He doesn't have to say anything. He just gives you a job in the ward nursery.

Other faiths probably have nurseries in their churches too, places where children go and play while their parents are off in Sunday School learning the gospel through osmosis. It's the one common ground the various faiths in this area have.

Mormon nurseries are worse because we traditionally have more children per family unit than other faiths. It's part of the unofficial "Spread the Faith Through Reproduction" program we've been practicing for years.

If you don't think so, take a peek at the ward roster in the bishop's office. Ward families have little symbols next to their names. These aren't ancient Nephite characters; they're military unit designations. Squad, platoon, company, battalion, etc. And since we stopped practicing polygamy as a rule, you won't see division and corps designations except on rare occasions.

Anyway, Mormons have lots of kids. Which explains why we also have a ward rehab program for ex-nursery workers. The average human being can only take so much screeching over vanilla wafers and Fisher-Price toys. When the mind goes, as it inevitably does, they give you a blessing and stick you in the high priest group. Or they make you the ward doorstop.

I can say these bad things about ward nurseries because I've done hard time in them, both as a demon child and a harried adult. As a toddler, I drove more than one nursery worker right around the bend to lip-flipping insanity.

I got my just desserts when, shortly after getting married and moving to a new ward, the bishop called my wife and me to be nursery workers.

As an ex-nursery con, it was easy at first. Then my wife made me leave the gun at home. She said it frightened the children. I said she was a convert and so what the hell did she know about being a Mormon nursery worker?

Without the gun (and the whip), we lasted four months. In some wards—especially around BYU and along the west side of Salt Lake—that's a record. Bishops there would kill to get that kind of mileage out of a nursery worker.

It was the noise that got to me. I could handle the mess, the cleanup, and the body fluids. I could even handle the perpetually late parents. But I couldn't take the noise. I can't vouch for the offspring of other faiths, but the average Mormon kid separated from its mom makes more noise than a Chihuahua being sucked through a Shop Vac.

Quitting was easy. We just walked into the bishop's office, flung our temple recommends on his desk, and told him we worshipped Satan now. A good man, he recognized the subtle signs of nursery burnout and agreed to give us new church jobs.

We should have stuck with the devil. Damnation would have been easier than what we got. We were called to work with the ward teenagers.

You want a bad church job, try working with the Young Men/Young Women. It's just like the nursery only these kids have driver's licenses and fully functional reproductive organs. Some of them even have their own guns.

Just a Church job

Did you ever stop to think how much the average LDS ward resembles an ant farm? Oh, calm down. It's not heresy to compare God's chosen to bugs. Jesus compared us to sheep, and where's the flattery in that?

Think about it for a minute. You've got a whole bunch of people/ants racing around, bashing into each other while trying to accomplish tasks that to the casual observer seem pretty pointless. Then, to make matters worse, God/somebody pokes the heap with a stick or drops in a dead beetle and everyone gets hysterical trying to figure out how to cope.

Unlike Mormons, an ant is a marvel of nature. It can lift a burden fifty times its own weight. That's because (a) the ant is built for it and (b) his infinitesimal brain is

programmed so that he's too stupid to recognize something as impossible or potentially injurious.

Mormons are smarter than that. There's no way you or
I would try dragging a 75,000-ton aircraft carrier back to
our basement, would we? That much wheat maybe, but
not the U.S.S. *Constellation.*

But you and I will take a twenty-five-hour-per-day
church calling and pretend that it's a wonderful opportunity to serve the Lord. Whether it really is a wonderful
opportunity depends on the success of the calling and
whether or not it drives you to a serious Word of Wisdom
problem.

Like ants, most Mormons don't know how to say "no"
to a church task. The stake president calls us up and
asks us to be the ward astrologer or second counselor in
the Foyer Quorum and the first thing out of our mouth is
"yes."

I'm not saying the first response should be "no," but
some investigation is certainly in order if, as a result of
the calling, your professional career will go down the
tubes and you'll only see your family for a few minutes
every other month.

I've made a personal practice of saying "maybe" to
church callings. "Maybe" isn't an up-front rejection of
God and it lets me stall while I try to find out just how
much of a glorious opportunity I'm being offered.

One of the first things I want to know is exactly how
many people turned down this call to serve before the

THE CALLING

bishop got around to asking me. If, for example, the number of people asked is the exact number of people who were willing to sell their homes at a loss in order to move from the ward in a hurry, I know that "maybe" ought to be "no" and perhaps even "hell, no!"

On the other hand, "maybe" is safe and it works. I've had church callings for years with the perfect understanding that maybe I'd do them and maybe I wouldn't.

For most Mormons, "maybe" usually ends up being "yes." That's how much like ants we are. We invariably take the calling because (a) we'd be guilt-ridden if we didn't, (b) it's a boost to the ego if the call is in a leadership position, and (c) because we love the Lord even though He's decided to torment us for the moment (His moment being roughly the equivalent of your life expectancy plus ten years).

When the Lord calls some people to certain positions, you never know if He's tormenting that particular person or the ward as a whole. You'll never know, either, because even though we're offered the chance to vote against that person, no self-respecting Mormon ever does. Which is probably as it should be. Things being what they are in the Church, sooner or later you'll get your turn to be the Home-Wrecking Counselor or something and you'll want everyone to sustain you.

All of this leads me to the conclusion that a terrific best-selling book for the LDS market would be one titled *101 Ways to Turn Down a Church Calling without Being Killed by Lightning on Your Way Home*. I'd start writing it this very minute if I didn't have so much church work to do.

*M*ormon *fight* *S*ongs

A lot of things put me to sleep in church. My personal favorite is the music. Ninety percent of all Church hymns sound like dirges sung by an anesthetized dairy herd. There's no pep to them, no beat or rhythm.

A few years ago, the LDS church redid its hymnal. At the time, I hoped we'd get some mainstream tunes and current lyrics. About the only blood-pumper we had until then was "Onward Christian Soldiers"—Christianity's version of a Wehrmacht marching song.

The new hymnal turned out horrible. There are still no real rockers, only New Age versions of what we had before—the sort of stuff the government would use to torment barricaded nuts like Koresh and Noriega. Hey, beam *Take courage, Saints, and faint not by the way* against the side of somebody's house for a couple of hours, and they'd do anything, including 100 percent of their home teaching, just to get you to cut it out.

Most of our gospel tunes have their origins in other faiths. In this tradition of borrowing from other sources I've come up with some fine tunes for the next hymnal.

Born to be Mild—A celestialized version of the old Steppenwolf hit, with such Church-approved lyrics as "Hit the temple running" and "Take the world in a modest embrace."

Leader of the P.E.C.—The Shangri-Las did the original in '64. The LDS version goes, "I met him at the chapel door!" backed up insipidly by "Yes, we get the Spirit."

Me and Bishop Agree—A gospel take-off of the only number one hit Janis Joplin ever had. Eight rambling verses about a disciplinary council that ends well.

There's Sussudio in my Soul Today—Phil Collins did the original. Re-mixed into an LDS get-down hymn perfect for closing songs even without the church-banned back-up saxes.

Strangers in the Right—An oldie hymn for those threatened by more pew-stomping practice tunes. A Sunday School crooner tune especially designed for mixed congregations of young and old. Also great for singles wards.

Mama Told Me (I Had to Come)—Inspirational Primary song originally done by Three Dog Night and remixed as a catchy reminder to youngsters.

Oh Thou Rock and Roll of Our Salvation—Joan Jett and the Blackhearts. Not a big favorite. Destined to be one of those tunes choristers love to make the entire congregation stand up and sing.

These Boots are Made for Tracting—"And one of these days these boots are gonna tract all over Yuma, Arizona." An MTC favorite.

Sunday, Sunday—Original sung by the Mamas and the Papas. Redone by the Church Correlation Committee to provide an upbeat look at modern Mormonism, with such lyrics as "Sunday, Sunday, can't rest that day . . ."

We're an American Church—Ripping Grand Funk tune. Rewritten for the express purpose of allaying foreign fears. "We're coming to your land, we want to be your friend, we're an American church." Okay, it doesn't rhyme, but neither do some traditional hymns.

Bad, Bad, Elder Brown—"You know the south side of Chicago is a godless side of town . . ." Another MTC favorite about the dangers of lusting in your heart.

Others...

Killing Me Softly with his Testimony.

Your Love Keeps Lifting Me High on a Mountain Top.

My Boyfriend's Back (ten months early).

Let's Get Spiritual.

The nephites strike back

Only about five hundred people called to tell me that I got the three degrees of glory mixed up after one of my columns ran in the paper. One of them was my mom. She told me to stop writing so late at night and cut out the Diet Coke because it was hurting my brain. Another was my bishop who said one more stupid mistake like that and I'd be going to summer Sunday School.

People are so sensitive about religion these days. Probably because it's becoming more and more of a commercial venture for them. You can't beat religious devoutness in some people if they've got a few bucks invested in their faith.

I'm talking about the commercialism of Mormonism here. Walk into some Salt Lake City stores and you'll see

Mormon literature, knickknacks, games, music, and diets. There are Mormon tie tacs, bumper stickers, posters, videos, and lots of other useless doodads.

The commercialism of Mormonism roughly parallels the world market, so it's only a matter of time before some Wasatch entrepreneur tries to market a temple for Barbie and Ken to get married in or a G.I. Joe version of the Nauvoo Legion or Manti Temple hubcaps.

Which means it's about time for me to come up with my own religious product line. As soon as I find twenty investors to kick in a million bucks each, I'm going to retire . . . ah, go to St. George and start developing some Mormon video games. Here's just a sample of what I'm working on:

NEPHI'S QUEST II—Help Nephi tunnel out of the Jerusalem City Jail after he's been arrested for mugging Laban. Extra points if you can convince Zoram to drop kidnapping charges.

SUPER MORONI BROS.—Players do their best to find gold in order to fashion more plates for the Book of Mormon. The player with the most gold plates wins—but the weight of the book may also impede his flight, allowing the evil Lamanites to run him down and horribly slay him, yea, even until he becomes extinct.

THE ONE AND ONLY—Help Molly enroll at BYU and search frantically for a husband. Highest score goes to player who can accomplish this in a single semester. No points for becoming engaged to current boyfriend's mission companion.

DONKEY KORIHOR—Convince poor Korihor to repent before he learns the hard way that handicapped pedestrians in the promised land do not have the right of way.

P.E.C. MAN—Can you make it to all your priesthood executive committee meetings, earn a living, and still get your home teaching done on time and in person? Can you locate a Maalox potion to get you through another ward correlation council meeting?

MS. PEC MAN—Two-player version of above game. One player sits behind the other and sweetly gives advice.

ZAP ZARAHEMLA—Which curse will work best on the mighty city of the Nephites? Can you bend the Nephites' stiff necks with a plague of boils or will you have to give up and park a mountain on them?

WHERE'S THE PLACE?—Elude the mobs and find a new place for Mormons to practice and commercialize the faith. Earn obedience points by fasting until you're invisible.

Invest now and avoid the rush.

Teenagers: a plague upon the land

As a Bible scholar of no small renown, I've long held the position that there was an unknown plague which caused Pharaoh to finally release the children of Israel into the desert.

Plagues of frogs, lice, boils, hail, and flies were certainly bad, but I believe it was the threat of a final plague that ultimately convinced Pharaoh that the Israelites were more trouble than they were worth.

Picture stubborn Pharaoh, his head lumpy with boils, sitting on his throne surrounded by dead cows and No-Pest strips. In comes Moses, who calmly announces the final measure of God's wrath.

"It shall come upon thee and thy house," Moses intones solemnly. "A plague of—teenagers."

Pharaoh promptly faints. The Israelites scoot into the desert where it takes them forty years to get their heads together.

I know what I'm talking about. A plague of teenagers has come upon my house. Frankly, I'd rather have lice. With all due respect to boils and rivers of blood, it just doesn't get any worse than living with teenagers.

Teenagers as a biblical plague is an important religious consideration because (a) no house can truly have the spirit of the Lord *and* a teenager at the same time, and (b) every house has or will have a teenager in it.

I haven't proven it yet, but I strongly believe that teenagers are the anti-Christ. Their behavior, music, dress, and speech are an affront to heaven.

Proof can be found in biblical parallels. We "know," for example, that hell is going to be full of rebellious souls, lots of shrieking damned, tormenting demons, and utterly devoid of peace. If that doesn't describe your average teenager's bedroom, then you haven't been around them enough to know.

My own teenagers are a sore trial to me, my wife, the neighbors and frequently the police. It requires an exorcism to get them to turn down their music or clean their rooms.

Church leaders are always harping about the proper rearing of children, claiming that if you do the right things, kids will make you and God proud.

Nonsense. It doesn't matter what you do because your

angelic little kids are eventually all going to become teenagers with screwed up hormones and evil desires. They'll dress like slobs, bad mouth authority, and listen to music loud and virulent enough to kill weeds. Nothing you say will matter to them, especially if it has anything to do with religious values outside of maybe satanic worship.

The only mercy involved in a plague of teenagers is that like all plagues which don't necessarily kill you, eventually it comes to an end. Teenagers grow into young adults and move away to attend school, get married, or go to prison. Peace returns to the home just as it did to Egypt.

Unlike Pharaoh, I can't figure out what I did to warrant this plague of teenagers. Probably something in my past that I don't remember. Sometime when I was totally selfish and insensitive to the needs of others, a time of demonic possession.

I asked my dad, but he just laughed.

LDS mother keeps things under wraps

If you spent $900 a month mailing cupcakes to Brazil, people in most places would think you were nuts. In Utah, they know you're just the mother of a Mormon missionary.

With 50,000+ missionaries in the field, Mormons have made the mailing of packages a religious rite. No other religion in the world spends as much money as we do to send Betty Crocker products to places that make Bedrock look futuristic.

It won't be long before the LDS church officially adopts the mailing of packages as a gospel ordinance. By the year 2,000, "Are you honest in your dealings with the post office?" will be part of the temple recommend interview.

Next to caffeine-free Diet Coke, mailing supplies are the hottest retail item in Utah. With all those sons and daughters in faraway places, nobody knows more about packaging than Mormon mothers. They've heard all the stories about the larcenous postal systems in other countries. There's no way Juan Valdez is going to pick his coffee beans in a BYU sweatshirt if they can help it.

Practice makes perfect. When an LDS mother wraps something, it stays wrapped. The Relief Society could give the drug cartels lessons in defeating snoopy postal inspectors. However, expert packaging skills do not necessarily mean that careful thought goes into the contents of a missionary package.

For some reason, mothers always send what they want you to have rather than what you actually need. You could be doing the Lord's work on the edge of the world's biggest swamp and do you think Mom's going to send you a can of insect spray or a bug zapper? No way. You'll get twenty-two pounds of rock-hard fudge and a back issue of the *Ensign*.

The weirdest thing anyone ever sent me was $50 worth of aerograms, those little blue sheets of paper that fold up into their own envelopes. Aerograms come pre-stamped so you can just pop them in the mail. They work great—if you mail them from America. In South America, U.S. aerograms are just blue sheets of paper with origami instructions.

No one ever sent me what I really needed in the mission field—dandruff shampoo, morphine, Pepto-Bismol, or a handgun. All I ever got was petrified brownies, Mormon Tabernacle Choir cassettes, and birthday cards the size of J.C. Penney catalogs

What is it with mothers that they have to spend twenty bucks to send a birthday card to their son living in a place even rats talk bad about? When it gets there, the son usually has to stand in line six hours and pay another ten dollars to get it. That's if he can get it at all. Some places are so backward that the arrival of a Hallmark card becomes

a village media event bigger than the time the headmaster's pig was shot by an army patrol.

Why not send money instead? You can wire it for dang near nothing. Best of all, the person getting it won't be subjected to a strip search in the local customs office when he goes looking for it. He can even use the money to bribe officials to let him go home without the requisite slapping around for bothering them.

Better yet, send yourself. On some airlines you can go see your missionary for less money than it costs to buy, wrap, send, and receive a package filled with love.

Born again Mormon

A few years ago, one of my close friends got "born again." In the interest of protecting his privacy, I'll refer here to John Allen McGee of Seattle, Washington, as "Bill."

A backslid Baptist, Bill married a very religious girl. He did what most men do in situations where they expect to get anything else—he got religion. Bad.

I visited Bill shortly after he renewed his faith in God and domestic harmony. Being close friends but members of different faiths, we immediately fell into a raging argument over the Sonics and the Jazz. Later, we calmly discussed the impact of religion in our lives.

"You can't be born again, stupid," Bill said. "You're a Mormon."

A self-taught religious scholar, I immediately had

Bill writhing in the crushing grip of my reason. "Can so."

Bill insisted that only real Christians could be born again, something that required a new look and a rededication to one's belief in God. Mormons, he said, were too dogmatic to accomplish something as radical as this.

It's true. Mormons can't be "born again" in the traditional sense. Outside of "becoming more active" or "re-baptized" we've got no label that indicates we've reexamined our religious commitments and emerged anew, as something different.

Until now. Enter "New Age Mormons." The term itself doesn't really mean anything. It just came to me once when, half asleep during a fast and testimony meeting, I slumped forward and hit my head on the back of a pew. While the parameters are fairly obscure, New Age Mormons tend to be broader, less intense, less gullible sorts of Mormons.

New Age Mormons are interested in the deeper meanings of Sunday School lessons. If, for example, Mormons are so big on obeying the laws of the land, how come we think it's cool that Nephi hacked the head off an unconscious drunk, burglarized his home, and kidnapped his servant?

New Age Mormons also tend to blend well with members of other faiths (except for Sonics fans). We don't believe that all non-Mormons are out to get us or that they can trace their genealogical roots back to members of the mobs that drove us out of Missouri and Illinois.

Likewise, New Age Mormons don't necessarily believe all the faith-promoting stories they read in the *Ensign*. New Age Mormons know that paying your tithing, going to church, saying your prayers, and having Family Home Screaming won't necessarily keep you from getting cancer, mugged, or audited. Shoot, they can't even guarantee an NBA championship.

New Age Mormons generally eschew trappings of Mormondom—wing tips, vinyl scripture covers, over-heated meetings, potluck dinners, and proud displays of the BYU block letter "Y."

New Age Mormons do not believe that weeping in a church meeting is a sure indication that the Spirit is present. Usually it means that you're scared silly to be baring your soul in front of a bunch of yahoos who are going to talk about you later.

New Age Mormons also know that if they push this new age stuff too far, they can actually have their falling and destruction made sure.

Faith promoting rumors

Faith Promoting Experiences. Every religion has them. Whether it's seeing the Virgin Mary, achieving Zen, or graduating summa cum laude from BYU, the devout rely on these experiences as inspiring affirmations of their faith. FPEs are the story problems of religion.

A generic FPE goes something like this: A family is starving to death. The father is terminally ill and can't work. Creditors are after them like a pack of wolves. The family doesn't know what to do except shiver and pray. Wouldn't you know it, one day an angel/the Virgin Mary, /a barefoot monk appears and writes them a huge check, taking care of all their money worries. Dad gets cured and becomes a seminary teacher/priest/itinerant karate instructor.

I've got no real problems with FPEs. Heck, as a Mormon I was raised on pioneer, missionary, and Relief Society FPEs. So, if someone lays claim to a personal FPE, I'm inclined to give them the benefit of the doubt even if it's something *Ripley's Believe It or Not* would be embarrassed to print.

Some people take FPEs to heart and say, "See what happens when you live right?" They rarely stop to think of the flip side of the experience. Namely that FPEs are very subjective. Ninety-nine times out of one hundred, life doesn't work out that way.

What about the other side of the coin? What about the people who listen to an FPE and say to themselves, "Hey, wait a minute. The wolves were eating me once and no angel came. What gives?"

See, the insidious message of FPEs is that if you're living right the Spirit will save you just as it did the people in the FPE. And that just ain't so. Odds are you're going to die of hunger, get robbed and beat on the head, or lose your business anyway. It's a fact that for every person whose cancer goes into remission because of an FPE, a million more people die.

If you aren't careful with FPEs, you'll end up bitter and mean and wondering why God doesn't like you as much as those people in the *Ensign* magazine.

The medical profession really takes it in the shorts when it comes to FPEs. Countless FPEs end with ". . . and when he/she went back to the doctor the very next day, the cancer/tumor/alien was gone." Listen to enough medical FPEs, and pretty soon you start to wonder if God didn't put doctors here just for comic relief.

A lot of Mormon FPEs are spread in testimony meetings. Most are pretty benign, personal claims to problems resolved by the help of the Spirit. However, some of them sound like they should have been narrated by Robert Stack. A few I've heard could double as *X-Files* episodes.

Another problem with FPEs is that if you start to see them as essential to your salvation, you start waiting for them. Pretty soon everything has FPE potential. Some FPE junkies are so far gone that there's no convincing them that some things in life just happen and you're supposed to make the best of it. They're so out of touch with reality that they could make an angelic visit out of getting bit on the neck by a rabid bat.

I don't think life was meant to be an FPE, not like you read about or hear on TV anyway. If you haven't had one in a while, I wouldn't take it personally.

it's Best *to* hope for the Least

I lost my church job Tuesday night. Bishop Smith called me down to the ward house and fired me. Then he turned right around and hired me as something else. In Mormon parlance this is referred to as a "release" and a "call."

I wasn't bothered by the change. The church job I had didn't pay anything and neither does the new job I've got. From bishop right on down to the kiddy wranglers in the nursery, LDS church jobs pay zip when it comes to actual money. The best you can hope for is to get a new church job that requires less effort than the old church job. I broke about even.

You're supposed to get blessings instead of money for doing your church job well. But ever since I heard a guy call the loss of both of his legs "a blessing," I much prefer the no pay plan. Complaining about no pay could get you blessed until your insurance company won't cover you anymore.

It's different in other churches. Some faiths actually interview and take resumes for various church jobs. Salaries and benefits are discussed. Relocation packages are offered. A friend of mine, a pastor in another church, actually got a raise in salary by transferring to a bigger congregation back East.

Most Mormons don't go looking for church jobs. It's considered *tres gauche* if not outright nuts for someone to actually aspire to be a bishop or a Relief Society president. Besides, the way things work in the LDS

church, eventually you'll get your turn whether you want it or not.

Those who don't understand the nature of an LDS church job wonder why people don't just say no when called to be something like the ward pack mule. Part of it's an honest desire to be of service to others. Part of it's guilt. It's hard to say no to your bishop when you know he's knocking down 20+ hours a week and all he wants out of you is to set up some chairs or teach a lesson to a bunch of bored folks.

Here's a quick list of LDS church jobs which, if a Mormon you know gets one, means a certain amount of consolation (preferably alcohol-free) is in order:

BISHOP—In charge of the spiritual needs of 200-500 people, some of whom have personal problems that will scare your hair white.

RELIEF SOCIETY PRESIDENT—Supervise the women's service auxiliary, which specializes in caring for the sick and hungry while at the same time making stuff like wheat chili and painted wooden bunnies.

ELDER'S QUORUM PRESIDENT—Responsible for priesthood holders between the ages of 18-40+—or the ward's free manual labor force. Great place for a union except that nobody can bust a strike faster than God.

PRIMARY PRESIDENT—Invariably a woman. No man, including an apostle, is spiritual enough to make hundreds of nasty little yard apes sing songs and sit still for two hours without hurting some of them.

SUNDAY SCHOOL TEACHER—A once a week job that should require the teacher to find a new and exciting way of presenting gospel principles the class has heard ad nauseam but invariably doesn't.

WARD MISSION LEADER—Responsible for seeking out new converts within the boundaries of the ward. Hard to do since most aren't interested in being baptized because it means they'd get a church job.

Weed my Sheep

The Bible is full of metaphors. One of the most common is the reference to Jesus being a shepherd. The New Testament refers frequently to the rest of us as his sheep.

This comparison is, I suppose, intended to illustrate our relationship with the Savior. He takes care of us, keeps the wolf (Satan) from getting us, and goes and looks for us when we get lost. Images of cuddly sheep and the kind shepherd make for good religious press.

However, I have this sneaking hunch that referring to humans as sheep wasn't intended entirely as a term of endearment. Only people who haven't worked with sheep would think that such a reference was entirely a kind or flattering one. Among real-life shepherds, sheep are renowned for being about as sentient as cement.

Why not tigers, huh? What's wrong with "the dolphins of Israel" or "false prophets in beavers' clothing?" After all, these animals have some respect. People admire their qualities and even name sports teams after them. How many fans do you think a football team called the "Jerusalem Sheep" would draw? It's almost insulting.

My personal choice for a metaphoric reference to the Lord's flock would have been elephants. They're big and strong and noble and no other animal messes with them without dire consequences. Elephants are scientifically proven to be smarter than 32.8 percent of all humans. Wouldn't it make God prouder to say "feed my elephants?"

Has anyone ever taught a sheep anything remotely close to a circus trick? Nope. All sheep know how to do is stand in the middle of the road, get sheared, and be eaten. They're the vegetables of the animal kingdom. Take a potato, cover it with wool and stick some legs on it, and you've got a sheep.

Which brings us to the real reason the scriptures refer to human beings as sheep—we're morons. Proof is in the way we behave. God gives us prophets, scriptures, a personal Savior, and we still act like we don't have two brains cells to rub together.

God tells us to be chaste and monogamous and when we aren't, venereal disease comes at us like a truck on the highway. Under those circumstances, only a sheep could be surprised by the rampant spread of AIDS.

God also tells us to be peaceful and loving and we aren't. You want stupid like a sheep? Check out the Crusades. People going around killing other people in order to convert them. Your average ewe seems like a Harvard math professor compared to this kind of human behavior.

Greed and larceny. You can't beat the 90s for sheep-like stupidity in response to this commandment. Most Yuppies would rather have a BMW than a personal relationship with God. It's little wonder we have a homeless problem.

So it goes with virtually everything God tells us. He can't leave us alone for two minutes without us wandering off a metaphoric cliff out of sheer stupidity. If He wasn't God, it probably would have driven Him crazy by now.

Fade to black

I've got a friend who says he's an atheist. I'm not sure if he is or not. Whenever Harv gets upset, he always says "dammit," which, if you think about it, is pretty stupid for an atheist to be saying. He never says, "Ah, fade to black."

Blackness is what atheists claim happens when you die, although some atheists might disagree with me here. In fact, there are probably varying brands of atheists just like there are different denominations of Christians. I'll probably get a letter from the congregational atheists who, unlike unholy roller atheists, claim blackness is really something rather than nothing at all and therefore isn't true atheism.

Harv and I have lots of arguments about religion. I

can't prove there is a God to his satisfaction and he can't prove there isn't one to mine. These are stimulating conversations, much better than the ones I get into in church where everyone just agrees until they fall asleep. I've never fallen asleep talking to Harv.

Harv says I'm going to be real disappointed when I die because I won't get a celestial reward like I've been promised. To which I reply that if there really isn't a God, I won't be feeling much of anything at all. If either of us is at risk here it's Harv. I'd rather cease to exist as a dead Christian than wake up on God's front porch some morning as a dead atheist. Talk about disappointments.

Christians like to beat up on atheists, sure in the knowledge that God will reveal himself to them someday through a horrible personal trial. The oft-repeated phrase "there are no atheists in foxholes" is intended to prove that people near death always turn to God, which not only isn't always true but is also a pretty stupid phrase. I mean what greater proof of an absence of deity is there than people running around killing each other wholesale?

I went through an atheist period when I was younger. It was mostly to annoy my folks but also because it felt good not to have someone looking over my shoulder whenever I thought bad thoughts or didn't behave like someone said I should. It was kind of liberating to be free of the old religious taboos I'd subscribed to all my life. But then I was only nine.

Harv's problem is that he wants to make the existence of God a math problem. Can't be done. There are too many variables for the human head to factor.

You just can't prove to someone that God exists. This understanding only occurs in the most private place a person has: his heart. It's an individual experience, one that can't be shared accurately with others who weren't there when it happened and didn't feel what you felt.

I found God in a grove of trees when I was thirteen. I didn't go there to pray or meditate. I went there to fish and instead blundered into a group of college girls skinny-dipping in the creek. Ten seconds changed my life. I've never doubted Him since.

Harv says this isn't real proof that God exists. I say Harv wasn't there.

Bible bash

Got a call from a gospel bully the other day. He phoned me up to flex his theological muscles. He was good at it too. First he told me that I was a ninety-pound doctrinal weakling. Then he shoved me down and kicked scripture in my face.

Happens a lot. Maybe it's because I'm not as versed as I should be in The Word, or more probably it's because there's an uncommon amount of Bible bullying going on out there.

I'd blame myself for being ignorant except for one teensy little thing. The gospel bullies fight amongst themselves more often than they pick on me. Devotion to their biblical barbells makes them about as intolerant of each other as it does me.

Actually, it's not just the Bible. Whether you're a follower of the Koran, the Tantra, Talmud, or Book of Mormon, you'll run into the prosecutors of the faith who use their book-learning like Dirty Harry uses a magnum.

But let's not confuse well-versed with well-intentioned. It's one thing to know your Bible et al. and another thing to grasp the meaning behind it. Being able to quote the book of Revelation verbatim doesn't make you a saint anymore than having a set of muscles makes you a champion of the downtrodden. It's all in how you use it.

Gospel bullies don't study the scriptures for the sake of helping their fellowman so much as they do it for the sake of proving that their fellowman is a geek of Satan. Being scripturally buff is a whole lot more important to them than being kind and considerate.

Fortunately, gospel bullies are easy to spot. Like a beach bully flexing his pecs, they'll work scripture references into every conversation they have with someone of a different faith. Forget the possibility of building bridges based on mutual tolerance and respect, what about Deuteriticus chapter 11, verse 185? Oh, yeah, well what about Famousamos 14:22?

I fell into this trap while serving an LDS mission in a small Uruguayan bog by the name of Pedo del Perro. Every morning on our way to the bus stop, my companion and I passed two Baptist missionaries, kids like ourselves out trying to save the world. And every morning, we sniped scripture at each other.

"Matthew 15:16," the Baptists would growl.

"Thessalonians 3:11," we'd fire right back.

My companion and I wasted hours studying the scriptures in order to participate in this biblical version of name-calling. In the long run, we probably would have been better off to start a fistfight with the Baptists just to get it out of our system.

The only person who got anything out of this brainless exchange was the devil. He probably thought it was as fun as, well, hell. Looking back, I regret that we didn't become friends with the Baptists. After all, we were basically after the same thing: to make people better. And they had a Frisbee.

I haven't flexed my scripture muscle in years and I don't plan on starting again. For one thing, people can prove just about anything in them if you try hard enough. If you don't think so, take a minute and count how many faiths there are from just the Bible.

That doesn't mean that reading the scriptures is a bad idea. But I have this sneaking suspicion that using the word of God to beat people up isn't exactly what it was intended for.

the Answer to most prayers

The first time I ever really prayed from the heart was when a furious black man threw me out of an airplane over Alabama. For years I thought the prayer worked because I lived.

I was in the army and the prayer was a desperate plea for God to save me despite a lifetime of evil behavior. What I wanted more than anything was for my parachute to open, carry me safely to the ground, and deposit me with no more than two or three broken bones. I remember promising God that if I lived and none of the broken bones happened to be my spine or skull, I would go on a mission or become a nun, I forget exactly. Hey, I was stressed.

My prayer wasn't very articulate. You won't find anything in Psalms or Proverbs to compare it to. It was a mentally yammered, "Oh God, oh God, oh God," as Sgt. Washington dragged me over to the door and bellowed for me to get my "ugly stupid self" off his airplane. Amen was a boot in the butt.

Most religions have a formula for prayer, a corporate approved method of conversing with God. The general feeling you get is that if it's not done exactly the way they say in church, God won't listen to your prayer or, at the very least, respond only grudgingly. Rubbish. When you're God, you listen to whomever you want.

I bet God listens to Pope John Paul every bit as much as He listens to President Gordon B. Hinckley. He no doubt listens to Billy Graham even more than He listens to me. Catholics, Methodists, Jehovah's Witnesses—God listens to the righteous no matter what card they're carrying.

Which brings up an interesting point. Namely, how righteous do you have to be in order for God to decide your prayers are worth answering? God has answered one or two of my prayers even though I've been a jerk my entire life. Despite years of coveting, lusting in my heart, and voting the Democratic ticket I've reached forty with a nice wife, an okay job, and all my arms and legs.

We'll probably never know exactly what the righteous/answered prayer ratio is. There are too many variables, not the least of which is what exactly constitutes an answer. Just because Sgt. Washington was never actually able to follow through on his oft-repeated threat of "killing me

another four-eyed white boy" doesn't mean God answered any of my jump school prayers. Too many really good people have prayed and died anyway for me to think that.

Answers to prayers come in a variety of shapes and sizes. From personal experience I can say that the predominant answer to prayer is "no." Another common answer is "none of thy business." One I got on my mission was "leavest thou me alone." This has led me to the belief that even though prayer is important and a must for maintaining a close relationship with our Creator, it isn't supposed to be used like some weepy call to a bail bondsman.

Trouble is what life is all about. Or, more correctly, how we deal with trouble. In that regard, prayer can help us cope, make us think, and even give us peace when we're 2,000 feet over Alabama.

Amen.

Missionary reunions *for* the *dead*

I went on an LDS mission a long time ago. Shortly after the Salt Lake Temple was completed, the Church sent me to labor in South America.

It was cool. In fact, if they'd let me take my wife and our big screen TV, I'd probably go again. But I'd rather be dead than go to another mission reunion. Mission reunions are the same no matter how long ago or where you went.

Invariably there's a sing-along (*"El arroyito da*, something, something, something . . ."), a slide show (. . . and this is Elder Lummox before he got stripped and beaten by that mob in Morzillo"), and a light buffet of things a doctor with an actual medical degree told you never to put through your colon again.

Only missionaries fresh home from the field actually enjoy mission reunions. It's a time for them to rehash the joys of carrying the gospel to places on earth where the inhabitants only recently stopped eating missionaries. They get to see who's married, who's going to BYU, and who still has the runs.

A mission reunion is a time for people to get together who still believe a mission was the "best two years" of their lives. It isn't the time for gospel mossbacks like me to relive the door-to-door glory days. Listening to kids sniffle about the "best two years" of their lives when they only recently emerged from puberty doesn't carry a lot of weight. I mean come on, what life?

None of this means that I'm anti-mission or that I don't remember my own mission fondly—parts of it, anyway. There's some serious character building that comes with living for six months in a third-world ghetto with a companion who has the personality of a fish stick and won't stop whining about the food and his girlfriend.

Stuff like that either makes you spiritual or drives you nuts. You just have to come back with an honorable release to find out which.

I have good memories of my own mission. Even though it's been a long time, I still remember part of at least one discussion. *"Hermano Gomez, usted y su familia se van a quemar horriblemente con el diablo."** Eh? Tell me I don't still got it.

---

* *Brother Gomez, you and your family are going to roast in hell with the devil.*

Best of all, I remember what it was like baptizing the Barbe, Grillo, and Valenzuela families; and how God finally answered my prayers and transferred Elder Clapfuddle to Nalgas de Vaca, where he got amoebic dysentery.

There were rough times, to be sure. Like the time my pet monkey, Sidney Rigdon, fell down the neighbor's well. And the time Elder Mutz got hit by a bus and had a vision that Elder Barndorf was the devil. Or the time we were broke and ate tripe for three straight weeks.

But memories of spiritual events aren't the reasons why people go to missionary reunions. No way. Missionary reunions are the LDS church equivalent of high school reunions. People only go to them to find out who got rich, fat, bald, breast implants, divorced, excommunicated, and/or sent to prison.

In a morbid way, it's kind of fun to see how all the people who were so obsessive about the gospel in the field turned out after twenty years of real-life application.

In my own two-year group from South America, most of us are still married. One of us, however, is a convicted bank robber (I'm not making this up), four of us became cops (two of whom eventually got killed), about three dozen of us are divorced, two are members of other churches, and at least three are openly homosexual. The rest of us are trying to cope with the spiritual devastation of rearing teenage children.

Even though I've vowed never to be caught dead at

another mission reunion, I have this nagging feeling that it's beyond my control. Missionary reunions are so popular among Mormons that they have more than passed into the realm of gospel tradition. It's only a matter of time before the Church officially adopts them and starts doing missionary reunion work for the dead.

Keeping *the* *m*ormon sabbath

IMPORTANT GOSPEL QUESTION: Are Sundays that fall in the middle of three-day weekends harder to keep holy than generic Sundays?

Before you answer, consider that three days is the minimum amount of time you'll need to pack up your stuff and head down to the lake and sunbathe until K.C. Masterpiece names you their poster child—and still make it back in time for work at, oh, say, noon on Tuesday.

The answer, of course, is none of your blinkety-blank business. Keeping the Sabbath Day holy is a personal thing 'twixt you and God. It hasn't been a group judged affair since the olden days when the Israelites enforced gospel stuff by threatening transgressors with extremely one-sided rock fights.

Today, Mormonites try to keep the Sabbath Day holy by pelting transgressors with opinions on what's not allowed. Some big Sabbath no-nos are no shopping, no movies, no reading of questionable books, no riding of dirt bikes, no hunting, no hitting family members with nail-studded boards. All of these things ostensibly detract from the Spirit.

With the exception of going to church, few Mormonites are as certain about permissible Sabbath activities. That's because appropriate Sabbath activities come in two seemingly conflicting versions: Sabbath stuff God actually cares about, and the stuff we do or don't do depending on how worried we are about what the neighbors think. It's simply amazing how many of us act like God grades on the curve.

Here's a list of generally accepted Mormonite Sabbath activities:

BLASTING DEER—"Deer huh-in" in Utah is a culturally permissible Sabbath activity occurring once or twice a year. Mormonites gather in genealogical units, say an opening prayer, and then fan out through the hills with the reverent intent of turning one or more of God's loveliest creatures into inedible jerky or dog food. NOTE: Poaching deer is never a proper Sabbath activity.

FAMILY DRIVES—Lots of Mormonite families take leisurely drives on the Sabbath. The operative word being "leisurely." A directionless and traffic-jamming jaunt up a canyon with the kids and the dog seems to be

" UNMIRING THE OX "... AN INCREASINGLY POPULAR SUNDAY ACTIVITY ...

OK, while a high speed run across the lake with rock 'n roll blasting from the stereo and two bikini-clad water skiers in tow is not.

VISITING FAMILY—Also OK. Especially if the family member is aged, lonely, and lives nearby. However, visiting a distant cousin who that Sunday just happens to be staying in a houseboat on Lake Tahoe is probably stretching it a bit. Truly blessed Mormonites have family members who need visiting in Vegas, Anaheim, Orlando, Honolulu, Cancun, or even Wendover.

READING—Church approved stuff is a safe bet, although a clean novel is also OK provided you can somehow relate the topic or the characters to the gospel. Try to imagine that Mr. Spock or the Sackett brothers will be getting the priesthood by the end of the book. Even bodice ripping romance novels make good Sunday reading if you can pretend that the missionaries show up at the end and teach the heroine the law of chastity.

Mostly, however, proper Sabbath reading refers to scripture study. Scripture study is an endorsed but seldom employed Sabbath activity that invariably leads to . . .

NAPS—A good way to stay out of most Sabbath trouble. The Utah-correct Sabbath nap requires that you loosen your pants, lie on the floor in front of the tube, and saw logs until the home teachers show up. Don't try

THE HOME TEACHERS

to catch a Sabbath nap while taking a Sabbath drive, though. Otherwise, it'll be cops, firemen, and paramedics who end up doing your work for the dead.

WRITING—This refers primarily to letters, journals, and the like. It doesn't include death threats to the IRS, extortion demands, letters to *Playboy* magazine, and salacious newspaper columns. And since I'm writing this on Sunday, I guess I better quit.

a Woman's place

The Vatican has decided to allow girls to stand before the altar as equals with boys. Heretofore a guy-only job, altar boy duties will now be shared with altar girls. The move is the latest by women who want to wrest traditional male-only church positions away from men. It's one more proof that the world is going to hell.

It's a well-known religious fact that women are more spiritual than men. Women dig church. In families of all denominations it's almost always the woman who makes the kids go to Sunday School and say their prayers at night.

Conversely, it's also a well-known religious fact that most churches are started and run by men. Buddha, Zeus, the Pope, Jesus, and Billy Graham are all men. So, if women are traditionally more spiritual and religion-oriented than men, how come they need men to start a church so they can have something to nag people about? Why don't they start their own?

As a religious theologian of no small renown, I say women trick men into starting religions. They have to because, biologically speaking, church is about as male-oriented as Tupperware and menopause. Church is women's way of controlling men by convincing them that they're needed in some role or another when we'd really rather be off getting bloody and filthy. You can't tell me that guys would intentionally set the Sabbath up on the same day as the deer hunt or the monster truck races. No way. It's women.

One of the sneakiest tricks women use in luring men into religion is going with their idea of depicting God as a male. This no doubt amuses women who, after years of picking up men's underwear and bailing them out of jail, know that portraying God as male is like classifying brussel sprouts as dessert. It just doesn't work. God is loving and omnipotent, whereas men are indifferent and incompetent. On good days.

If male gender can be assigned to anyone in the next life, it has to be the devil. There's no character reach here. I mean only a guy could think up something like hell. "So then we'll have lots of burning and screeching. Oh, and pitchforks. Bob, you were going to check on demons and imps. How's it coming, bro?"

Likewise, only women would think up something like heaven: golden thrones and angels and Enya tunes in the background. Ditto flowing robes, beatific looks, and doilies on every cloud. Not a speck of dust anywhere. Sort of like an LDS Relief Society homemaking night, only with better handicrafts. "Did you make that lovely halo yourself, Beatrice?"

Heaven is a chic place. You won't be able to belch, put your feet up, or leave your underwear on the kitchen floor. You certainly won't be able to hang out with your buddies because they all went to hell where there's cool stuff to do. Besides, you have to practice your harp.

Women better be careful in the good vs. evil struggle. Take away men's "need" to be in church and there's no telling where we'll end up.

Mormon *n*ones

If I wasn't a Mormon, I'd probably be Catholic. Theology aside, I'd feel more comfortable being a Catholic than a Baptist, a Druid, an Adventist, or a Rastafarian. At least I would as long as I didn't have to go to parochial school where nuns pulled my ears, slapped me with rulers, or beat me with nail-studded boards.

For most non-Catholics, the image of a nun as a grim taskmaster and disciplinarian is all we've got to go on. Nuns to us are straight out of *The Blues Brothers*, tormentors of children, women to be feared and avoided at all costs.

The only nun I've ever personally known was a teacher's aide at the elementary school I attended in

Spain. I can't remember her name, only that she was pretty and kind and never once gave in to a nun-like temptation to use a ruler or a cat o' nine tails on me.

Most people don't know that the LDS church has nuns too. We do. Only our nuns are spelled n-o-n-e-s, as in "none of this" and "none of that." The word actually originated in 1847 when, crossing the prairie, Mormon women were frequently asked by their husbands how much food was left and what the chances were of fooling around in the handcart on a given night.

SISTER MARIANNE PRUITT OF THE FRESHLY BAKED BREADS

More than a difference in spelling exists between Catholic nuns and Mormon nones. Whereas Catholic nuns are required to be celibate, Mormon nones are encouraged and even commanded to get hitched with earthly husbands in order to crank out as many children as possible, thereby compounding their blessed sorrow upon the land.

There are four basic orders of LDS nones.

Sisters of the Holy Handicrafts. This is a laboring order of nones that offers up its energy and time solely to Relief Society crafts. It's a reclusive order, one that eschews earthly politics, philosophy, and even basic common sense in order to pursue a life of fuzzy quilts and ceramic animals.

Sisters of the Bleeding Hearth. These are homemaking nones. Their entire lives are devoted to housework, food storage, money management, and keeping future bishops and apostles out of juvenile court until they're old enough to go on missions. Of the four orders, this is perhaps the most productive and beneficial to God's children. My mom belonged to the Bleeding Hearth but took Order of Holy Handicrafts vows after the kids left.

Sisters of the Wailing Womb. Procreative nones, their sole purpose for existence is to function as human teleport facilities between here and heaven. They are not celibate. On the contrary, these good sisters have an average of 11.5 children each and can easily be startled into full-blown labor on the shouted command of "Energize!"

Sisters of the Angry Apostlette. This is a more liberal order of nones. Previously known as Harridans of the Livid Fury, these sisters have challenged the ruling order by demanding priesthood equality and greater recognition of Mother-in-Heaven. Angry Apostlettes tend to be better educated and higher in profile than other nones. They're also the order that risks having a single word stamped on their individual church membership records. None.

Working *the* *ward* beat

When it comes to having a church job, you just can't beat being the person in charge of the congregation's newsletter. Do it right and it will be the shortest church job you ever have. I know because I was the ward person in charge of the newsletter once. For about forty-eight hours.

I don't know how it is in other faiths but Mormons don't use the word *editor* in reference to the person in charge of the ward newsletter. Instead, we call them "the person in charge of the ward newsletter." *Editor* denotes a person of some authority, and there's only one of those in an LDS ward.

"I want you to remember a couple of important things about ward news," Bishop Smith said when he asked me to take over the job.

"Can I quote you?" I asked.

Bishop Smith was no idiot. He went straight off the record. Paraphrased, his counsel was:

*God doesn't give a hoot about the First Amendment.

*A scoop is something used to dish up ice cream.

*Libel is what the bishop's wife says it is.

*The nursery is a way worse job than the ward newsletter.

Undaunted by these challenges, I went straightaway to work on the first—and last—issue of the 8th Ward Alternative Free Expositor.

Most ward newsletters are brainlessly simple. The content is limited to birthday announcements, quilting bees, mission calls, and Amway ads. Sometimes there's a cartoon and game section for kiddies.

I thought the ward was ready for something else. Something like "investigative ward newsletter journalism." It's a trade term, coined by me, which refers to the printing of information most people prefer to exchange behind one another's back.

The first—and last—headline of my newsletter was "Bishop 'a Chauvinistic fathead' says Sister Jones."

Then there was the advice column. Popular in other publications, it didn't fare as well in the newsletter. Everyone knew the "anonymous" people writing to "Dear Sister" about their personal problems. The good brother who wrote in about desiring the Relief Society

president still won't come back to church.

I also tried a cartoon strip titled "The Fire Side" which featured offbeat humor about talking cows going on missions, etc. Gary Larson came out of retirement long enough to threaten a billion dollar lawsuit.

I even tried a singles connection feature. Didn't work. The three singles we had in the ward already knew enough about each other to know they weren't interested. "SWMV seeks SWF who dang well better be a V" was the only submission I received.

My ward food review, "How to Garnish Military MREs," was a big flop.

The final straw was probably the plans for a swimsuit edition. I thought it would drive up circulation. It worked. When he heard about it, Bishop Smith's circulatory system blew a valve. He ordered descendants of the Nauvoo Legion to go up into the ward library and throw the photocopy machine out the window.

We met later. Bishop Smith said he didn't feel good about putting me to work in the nursery even though I deserved it. He just couldn't do that to kids. He did say that I'd never be successful printing such salacious and unflattering things about my fellowman.

I don't know. It got me this job.

Changing of the guard

My ward recently changed bishops. Short of finding out the Church isn't true, swapping bishops is the most traumatic thing that can happen to an LDS ward. That and maybe the death of Rush Limbaugh.

It happened all of a sudden. Our old spiritual leader, Bishop Smith, finally moved away. He was so concerned about disrupting our schedules that he tried to move in the middle of the night. In fact, he got a restraining order to keep the ward from getting within a hundred yards of his house.

For two weeks, every priesthood-bearing male (except *moi*) was suspected of being the new bishop. Prayers were said, testimonies offered, bets made, but no one knew for sure.

Stupid Mormons. I had the new bishop figured out two weeks in advance. I wasn't praying about it either. I was ice fishing. Don Bone and I were eating jerky and slowly freezing to death beside a hole augured in the middle of Fish Lake when suddenly he said:

"Darn."

"What?" I asked in surprise.

Don tried to act like nothing had happened. He pointed at the hole. "I said 'darn.' The fish got away."

Right then I knew. It wasn't what Don had said, but what he hadn't said.

"*Darn?*" I demanded. "What the hell is *darn?* Are you trying to stop cussing?"

"No."

"Liar. Prove it. Say *&#@!"

Don, the only guy I knew who could cure cancer just by cussing, wouldn't say *&#@! No matter how much I tormented him, the worst he would say was "flip." That and hit me in the head with the bait box four times.

By midday, Don had finally confessed that he was trying to quit swearing—and that he was going to be my new spiritual leader. He swore me to secrecy when I quit laughing an hour later. "You have to promise you won't tell anyone," he said.

I bowed my head, folded my arms, and promised.

I told everyone as soon as I got home. I mean I called people I didn't even know. My wife stopped me from taking out an ad in the newspaper. I explained that

I was doing Don a favor. A bishop has to get used to being lied to.

It's been six months and I'm still not adjusted. I was comfortable with the Fisher of Fish Don. I don't think I'll ever be ready for the Fisher of Men Don.

When your bishop asks if you've been honest in your dealings with your fellowman, it's a little hard to answer yes when he personally knows you once took 152 fish over the limit and that you consider dynamite to be an acceptable lure.

Likewise, it's hard when someone with whom you once held long, philosophical discussions about the differences between sisters in the ward and *Playboy* bunnies asks if you've been keeping your thoughts pure.

And it's especially hard on the ego when the bishop's response to the majority of your answers in the temple recommend interview is, "OK, now tell me the truth, you lying sack of spit."

It's also hard to say no to a bishop who routinely confuses "exhorting" with "extorting." Two months ago, Bishop Bone gave me a church job harder than nuclear physics. He said the Spirit directed him not to tell my wife certain things if I'd just say yes.

I hate my new bishop.

if *I* was *the* bishop

I took a lot of heat the past few days for saying that I hate my new bishop. This despite the explanation that for the next four to five years, I'm stuck fishing with a bishop rather than a friend. I still bear solemn witness that it stinks.

A lady from Midvale wrote to tell me that I was wrong and full of "damnation." She made another valid point. "If you're so smart, why aren't you the bishop?"

Contrary to popular local belief, there is no scientific correlation between being a bishop and being smart. In fact, all of my past bishops expressed frequent regrets that they weren't smart enough to avoid being my bishop in the first place.

Bishop Kirby. Sounds ominous. So do the titles Prime

Minister Kirby, President Kirby, Boss Hog Kirby, Surgeon General Kirby and Hillary Kirby. My wife says it's the juxtaposition of implied power and known fool in each of these titles that makes them so worrisome. I say she has even less of a chance of becoming bishop than I do, so she should shut up.

I think I'd make an interesting bishop. Not necessarily a good one, but at least not a boring one. Not like a certain ex-fishing buddy turned bishop that I know. So, just in case the stake president is thinking about making another change in the führership of the Dogpatch 8th Ward, maybe I ought to highlight my plan.

First, let's show for the record that within the confines of an LDS ward, bishops wield some serious power. The job doesn't pay diddly, but they have lots of say. Here's what Bishop Kirby would do with that say:

*Verily and henceforth, each and every testimony offered on fast Sunday will be followed by a three-minute question and answer period. Anyone who claims the Three Nephites helped them change a flat tire better have some proof.

*No excommunications for dissenting views in the Dogpatch 8th Ward. Anyone who doesn't think the way Bishop Kirby does has to hand-auger holes in the ice at Fish Lake. Dissidents can sulk, carp, hold forth, and pontificate all they want as long as they keep drilling.

*Currently, the average ward sacrament meeting sounds like feeding time in a rain forest. All small children (pew monkeys) must now wear muzzles in the chapel.

*Casseroles, Spam, Kool-aid, Jell-O, dry cookies, and lima beans are now against the Word of Wisdom. However, Diet Coke is still an optional item.

*A reinstatement of the two-and-a-half-minute talk and an introduction of the new and long awaited one-minute testimony.

*Let's not kid ourselves that the 8th Ward is a democracy. Long-winded correlation meetings are out of here.

*Gospel Essentials Ad Nauseam, a new Sunday School class for lifelong Mormons who need basics like baptism, prayer, tithing, and home teaching repeated nine hundred times before they sink in, will be held in the parking lot.

*Basketball and softball will be replaced by hockey and boxing as ward sports. At least then there will be an excuse for the behavior.

*Up-to-the-minute sports scores will be electronically posted on a board in the chapel near the hymn numbers.

There you have it, my plan for being a bishop. It's an interesting plan. Like most interesting plans it will never come to pass. That's good. Being a bishop would interfere with my fishing.

in Heaven there are no kids

I live in a young neighborhood. In the six houses surrounding mine, there are thirty-two children under the age of twelve. I know them all because I have a trampoline in my yard and because I try to earn a living at home.

Approximately two hundred times a day, a mucous-covered urchin will knock on the window of my office and ask, "Can we jump on yo twamp?"

If I say no, the little yard rats run away wailing like I'd tried to kill them and barely missed. If I say yes, the entire neighborhood gathers around back and proceeds to fight, scream, get hurt, throw up, and litter my yard with socks and half-eaten PBJ sandwiches.

It's no better in church. You simply can't feel the Spirit in a meeting when at least a third of the congregation is hooting and screeching and banging around between the pews like a bunch of alarmed apes.

I've raised children, lived around children, tended other people's children, and even been a child myself. I know that children are evil. Children are to a peaceful and enjoyable life what the Goths were to Roman social order.

Maybe kids were different during Jesus' time. Maybe 2,000 years ago children were models of decorum. Maybe during the New Testament kids weren't allowed to wire themselves to the max on sugar. It's the only reason I can think of as to why Jesus would want people to "become as little children."

Of course the orthodox will respond to this heresy by first insisting that I ought to be stoned, and, second, by claiming that what Jesus really meant was for us to become as humble and dependent on Him as little children.

Maybe. Maybe not. I've personally never understood why humble should be the first thing that comes to mind in connection with children. Ninety percent of the time they're loud, obnoxious, inconsiderate, destructive, and about as humble as French waiters. In fact, just about anything is more humble than a kid. A hydrogen bomb is meek and unassuming compared to the kids jumping in my backyard at this very minute.

So why not a better analogy? Why not become as little possums? They're cute and shy. How about as little

THE CRYING GAME

kittens? As little chicks? Little lemurs? Baby sloths. Ducklings. Really small rocks.

Hold on. Maybe Jesus meant for us to become exactly what adults become anyway: big versions of little kids. After all, the only person less humble than your average nose ranger is your average adult.

Adults. Everything I've said about children is true of adults. We're just more sophisticated about it. What's the

United Nations if it isn't one big clubhouse where some kids gang up on other kids? What's welfare if it isn't a bunch of kids yammering for Mom to make them a PBJ? Deadbeat dads are just grown up kids promising Mom that they'll take out the garbage later.

However, I'm sure Jesus knew what He was talking about even if I don't. There's bound to be a message of salvation in "become as little children" even if I'm too small-minded to get it. I'll just have to keep working on it even though it's a disturbing comparison. For that, I'll have to use faith.

Right now, I'm having faith that there are no kids in heaven.

Secret blood rites

Draw closer. I'm about to tell you a Mormon secret. Here it is: Believe it or not, the LDS church still uses blood in one of its rituals. It's a sinister, grueling affair accomplished only with a lot of groaning and screaming. It's called ward basketball.

For those unfamiliar with Mormon culture, ward ball is one of our darker secrets. It's the modern day equivalent of the Mountain Meadows Massacre.

The main purpose behind the Church's sports program is one of fellowshipping. The Church hopes people will use sports competition as a bonding experience. It works. There's nothing that draws people closer together quite like lusting after each other's blood.

Mormon roundball is divided into three degrees of

glory. First, there's Young Men's ball, comprised of kids between the ages of 12-18. Here, impressionable young men are introduced to the mechanics of sportsmanship, team cooperation, and cursing.

Unofficially, ward ball is also supposed to instill in young LDS kids basic street survival skills. Ward ball is to Mormons what tae-kwon-do is to Koreans. Mormon kids will need these skills when they're called on missions to places so rough and obscure that even the angels have to look them up in an atlas before fearing to tread there.

The second degree of ward ball glory is the varsity ward team. These are 18-30-something priesthood holders, pseudo-jocks with intense attitudes about the celestial nature of ward ball. These guys shoot hoops as though Bill Laimbeer and Dennis Rodman have had their callings and elections made sure.

Second-degree ward hoopsters are skilled in two areas of roundball glory: the laying on of elbows and the bellowing of insults nasty enough to hurt the feelings of Gadianton robbers. To them, fellowshipping comes after the ball game. It's what they do to make up for being such an overly competitive jerk that they fouled out in the first quarter.

Finally, there's the "veteran team," or third degree of ward ball glory. The term "veteran," of course, is a polite euphemism for older Mormon men. These are guys long past their roundball prime, guys who can't hold a

full-court press for longer than a minute without resorting to the sacred ward ball ordinance of trodding on tongues.

To have a real veteran team, the starting five alone should be high priests and represent roughly half the total body fat of the entire ward.

Unlike the priesthood, ward ball is not exclusively the domain of LDS men. Mormon women shoot hoops too. However, as it is with gentile roundball, few people pay any attention to women's sports. This has less to do with female sports skills than it does with the female attitude about sports.

Mormon women almost never take ward ball seriously. For them, sports isn't an episode of bloody religious *jihad*. Throw a few elbows in a women's game and they don't start a fight that requires a bishop and a firehose to break it up. They'll just trash your hair behind your back next Sunday. Where's the spiritual entertainment value in that?

As mean-spirited and nasty as it sounds, ward ball behavior has its roots set deep in the LDS faith. Ultrasecret modern day revelation indicates that the war in heaven started at a ward ball game.

Sniffing out the Sinner

Twenty years ago, I was waiting for a bus on a street corner in South America with three other LDS missionaries. Just as the bus arrived, an old man came scurrying up to the stop carrying an enormous load. In his mouth was a freshly lit cigarette. During the jostling to board the bus, the cigarette was knocked out of his mouth. He stood there with his arms full, staring disconsolately at his lost smoke.

At the time that it happened, I remember thinking "bummer." I was only about 18 months off of a bad cigarette habit myself and so I knew exactly how the old guy was feeling. That's when I did something awful. I bent down, picked up the cigarette, and stuck it back in his mouth. He thanked me.

I sat next to the old guy on the bus. He told me that he was working to support his son's family because his son had been arrested years before by the military and hadn't been seen since. The only other thing I remember about him was that he had a grandson named Ernesto who could play soccer like the wind.

This isn't the kind of gospel story that you'll find in a Church magazine. I didn't baptize this guy. He didn't run up to me on Temple Square twenty years later to tell me that I changed his life and he was now an LDS mission president. He more probably worked himself into the ground and died of cancer, a committed Catholic and family man.

The moral of this story was that I got in trouble with the zone leaders. They were mad that I had "disgraced the Church" by picking up the guy's cigarette. They said it gave the people who saw me do it the wrong idea about Mormons, the Word of Wisdom, and probably the Republican Party. As punishment, they sent me to labor in Labios de Perro where I fooled them and had a great time instead.

It's no secret that Mormons are down on smoking. So down, in fact, that we've made smoking a sin equivalent to child abuse and liberal politics. It's not hard to sniff out a smoker or a drinker in a crowd of Mormons because the smell conflicts with the predominant odors in an LDS chapel: baby lotion, dry cleaning, and bad breath.

It's too bad that other "sins" don't smell as strongly as

tobacco. Christians probably wouldn't be so smug if they did. Smoking might even become the relatively minor problem that it is if intolerance and arrogance simply smelled like a dead cat.

How about being selfish? What if being stingy and mean smelled like, oh, say, the dump? Or, better yet, raw sewage? How'd you like to sit next to someone in Church with a chain-stingy habit?

What if impure thoughts smelled like you had a three-week old carp hanging around your neck? You could, I suppose, tell your wife that the smell came from being with your friends instead of your own impure thoughts. And if gullibility smelled like garlic or a wet dog, you'd know immediately if she believed you.

Even sniffing these smells could get you in trouble. It could lead to passing judgment on others. Things could get really confusing if being judgmental smelled like spoiled milk. The smokers would be laughing at us.

The best we can hope for is that God has a better nose than we do.

Fellowshipping the angel of death

Last week, I was invited to speak to a group of funeral director's wives at the Salt Palace. Why I got picked to speak to such a group is still something of a mystery. I don't know what they were expecting. Personally, I expected something along the lines of a room full of Morticia Addams. Instead, the ladies were a really nice bunch. Like Republicans, only happier.

Since the talk—which must have gone OK because I haven't been sued—I've been thinking a lot about death. If I was wrong about funeral director's wives, maybe I've been wrong about dying. It could be nice.

Like most people of a religious bent, I've long had mixed emotions about death. Some of my nervousness stems from the fact that I haven't always lived a good life.

I haven't even sometimes lived a good life. OK, actually I've really only had occasional good moments. Maybe four. None recently.

So it makes sense that I'm afraid of dying. Part of this fear stems from the way death is presented in the Bible. Death is a good thing for prophets and martyrs (approximately .05 percent of the human race) and a bad thing for sinners (you, me, and everyone else). When saints and martyrs die, Jesus and angels show up to get them. When people like me die, it's the (ominous drum roll) Angel of Death.

I figure I'll check out in one of two ways: in a hospital bed absent some necessary organ or lying on my driveway clutching a snow shovel. Either way, one minute I'll be doing something else and the next there will be the Angel of Death. I hope he or she isn't real scary looking. Dying is bad enough without it being something like the worst trick-or-treat experience you ever had.

While meeting the Angel of Death probably isn't a lot

DEATH TAKES A HOLIDAY WITH HIS GOOD BUDDY BOB.

of fun, *being* the Angel of Death would be way cool. Especially if God gave you a lot of latitude about who had to die and when. If death really is a wonderful relief from life's woes, you wouldn't want someone like me as the Angel of Death. There are people I'd keep alive for 9,000 years. In fact, the more they whined, the longer I'd let them live.

The best part about being the Angel of Death would be killing your friends off. Calm down. Think how great it would be to have the Angel of Death be your best friend instead of something like the Grim Reaper.

Personally, I'd be in seventh heav. . . well, really jazzed if, when I died, the Angel of Death was my high school buddy Bruce Hepworth, who died of cancer in 1990. Death would be great if Hep showed up to get me. I know that somehow he'd make it fun. Then again, he might make me wait 9,000 years just for laughs.

On the other hand, some people say that dying is just like going home. If it is, it has to be like going home when you're married. Think about it. The minute you step through the door, somebody is on you with a bunch of demanding questions for which, if you don't have the right answers, you catch hell.

I think death is like getting fired from a job you should have quit in the first place. Afterwards, when you see how much freer you are, you don't know why you ever made such a fuss about it in the first place.

Marketing *the* faith

A couple of months ago, I was in K-Mart looking for a bath mat when I stumbled onto something even better: shot glasses and beer mugs with the Salt Lake Temple embossed on them.

Maybe it was the ironic juxtaposition of holy edifice and devil's swill that piqued my interest, or maybe it's just that I'm a sicko. Anyway, I bought a set of shot glasses. That night, I introduced my kids to a new Kirby family tradition—root beer shooters.

Root beer shooters didn't catch on with the kids as fast as my Family Home Evening poker nights. Try a shot of A&W with salt and you'll see why.

I was starting to think that the temple shot glasses were just an evil waste of money when my wife allayed my fears. Now that I'm on a diet, she says the glasses are the perfect serving size for root beer floats.

I went back to K-Mart a few days later looking for some temple beer mugs and temple champagne flutes. They were all gone. I thought it was because they had sold out but a clerk told me the glasses had instead been pulled from the shelves. Seems a bunch of do-gooders had complained that the glassware was offensive and, in a burst of Christian spirit, threatened to burn down the store.

Rather than deliberately baiting Mormons, I suspect the maker of these glasses was really just slapping something together to sell to tourists. The Salt Lake Temple was chosen as a logo because it's synonymous with Utah. It was just a poor (but funny) marketing idea. Sort of like you and I deciding to market Ayatollah brand pork rinds in Iran. We wouldn't necessarily be bad people, just ignorant and probably dead.

It's not like Mormons don't make a lot of religious kitsch themselves. I've seen Article of Faith key chains, Mormon prophet card games, Mormon pioneer board games, missionary pillows for girls to hug until their elder gets home, Mormon tie tacks, Mormon license plate frames, and even BYU beer kegs. OK, I went too far with the last one. The rest, however, are socially accepted religious kitsch currently on the LDS market.

I should get in on it. Over the years, a number of people have expressed interest in the set of leather Jimi

Hendrix scripture covers I had made in South America. One elderly sister even screamed in the middle of sacrament meeting when she saw them lying next to her on the bench. Maybe I'm being selfish by not sharing this kind of stuff with consumers.

Don't start sending me money just yet, but I've got serious plans for the following Mormon merchandise:

*14-karat gold-plated statue of Moroni cigarette lighters.

*General Authority pogs and slammers.

*Keep better track of the gentile in your life with a Porter Rockwell rifle scope.

*Gaddianton Robber action figures.

*Spare yourself a trip to the pulpit: "Is it live or is it Record-a-Mony?"

*General Conference "Spirit of God" World Tour jackets and T-shirts.

*Glow-in-the-dark plastic dashboard effigies of popular Book of Mormon prophets.

*Liahona compasses for motor homes and boats.

*RUPUR2? Personalized temple recommend license plates.

*"This Is the Place mats."

*Healthy, vitamin fortified Mormon-O's.

Shades of darkness

How's your spiritual health? Mine's not too good. A woman from Bountiful wrote to me last week, telling me that I was filled with the spirit of darkness.

I should probably get my darkness checked. It's been awhile. Like cholesterol, you don't want to let your darkness level get too high. Although there are some similarities between the two, darkness differs from cholesterol in one major area. The effects of high darkness don't go away when you die. In fact, they get lots worse.

Measuring your darkness level is almost exactly like measuring your cholesterol. The lower the better. A cholesterol level of 140 is pretty good. The average bucket o' lard American is about 230. A ranking of 300+ is seriously bad. Higher than that and your blood could be used to cook French fries at Wendy's.

The last time I had my darkness level checked, it was a whopping 245. Or so my bishop said. I had to take his word for it because, like cholesterol, you can't really measure your own darkness level. It has to be done by an expert. Someone like a religious leader, a parent, or a mother-in-law.

The highest my darkness level has ever been is 277. That's bad, real bad. Sheesh, Hitler was only a 305. Judas Iscariot was 352. Obviously, I had to do something about it. I was risking a full-blown damnation attack.

I started living better. Exercising my faith, saying my prayers, going to church, and switching political parties helped. I cut back on evil thoughts, cancelled my *Playboy* subscription, and stopped wishing certain people would die of gangrene. After a year or two, I got my darkness level down to 215.

Now I'm back up to 245. Sadly, I've come to realize that darkness is always going to be a struggle for me. I'm not like other people who naturally have low darkness levels. My spiritual nature is different than, oh, say, my friend Anne who has a 128 darkness level. And she doesn't even go to church. Like cholesterol, darkness isn't fair.

If you haven't had your darkness level checked in a long time (if ever) you really ought to have it done. You can't rely on appearances alone. I know a few religious people whose darkness levels are 290+. I also know at least one drunk with a darkness level that's almost in the double digits. That's pretty low. St. Francis of Assisi was only an 89. Moses was a 75. My mom is a 62.

While I'm no expert, I've put together this little chart to show where your darkness level might be. If it's high, you better take care of it. Pray or something.

350-300—Imminent damnation risk. Symptoms: stockpiling weapons and starting your own racist cult, genocide (all sizes), worshipping Satan, and thinking you're more special to God than literally everyone else.

299-250—High risk. Symptoms: ignoring the poor, bigotry, greed, blatant Republicanism, and a belief that God grades on a curve.

249-200—Fair. Symptoms: snobbery, narrowminded-ness, being selfish, sassing your mom, and a liberal arts degree from the University of Utah. OK, I'm kidding about your mom.

199-175—Good. Symptoms: tolerance, good deeds, caring about others. Infrequent self-indulgence. Rare bursts of anger.

174-125—Excellent. Symptoms: A life committed to the well-being of others.

124-75—A saint. People weep with joy when they hear your name. Your best friends are lepers.

74 -50—Get out of here.

Playing chicken with Heavenly Father

Last week, as a demonstration of my unwavering faith in God, I thought I'd pitch a tent and sleep on the freeway.

Sounds crazy, I know, but listen. I figured there's no way God would let a Peterbilt run over me unless it was supposed to happen anyway. It would be a wonderful example of faith to others.

I was all set to put this gospel plan into action when I read an Associated Press story in the *Salt Lake Tribune* about a fifty-six-year-old Oregon man who starved to death in his snowbound truck waiting for God to rescue him.

DeWitt Finley got stuck November 14 while taking a scenic route over the Klamath Mountains. Rather than walk sixteen miles to rescue, DeWitt Finley sat in his truck and wrote letters to his boss and family until he died, sometime after Jan. 19.

"I have no control over my life," Finley wrote. "It's all in His hands. His will be done."

A police official said that Finley, who spent most of his life in Southern California, was in "unfamiliar circumstances"—a situation referred to by the rest of us as "life."

Five months after getting stuck, Finley's corpse was found by teenagers. The kids were stuck too, but being your typical pagan teenagers they decided to hike out rather than wait for a proper Christian rescue.

Call me weak, but I immediately cancelled my plans to sleep on the freeway. Not because I don't have any faith in God, but because it's entirely possible that this particular gospel lesson would later become known as the Parable of the Roadkill.

What is it about religion that relieves some people of all responsibility for their actions? I mean where does it say that God takes care of people who refuse to take care of themselves? Heck, no wonder He calls us his sheep. I'll bet only opposable thumbs kept us from being covered with wool.

If God had wanted DeWitt Finley, it would have been a lot simpler to kill him with a heart attack in his sleep at home. That way, his boss, his family, his fiancée, and about two hundred cops wouldn't have spent five months worrying and looking for him. Who knows, maybe they were having religious experiences too.

By abusing this "Thy Will Be Done" religious logic, literally anything can be interpreted as God's will. What if I decided to spend the rest of my life shooting Spotted Owls? Who's to say (besides the Sierra Club) that it isn't God's will? Hey, if God wants the owls to live, He'll make them really hard to hit, right?

Maybe, but probably not. More than likely, God's will would be that the federal government should track me down and put me on trial for ten times as long as DeWitt was stuck in the mountains. No thanks. I'd rather starve to death than be a key player in the Parable of the Bickering Attorneys.

I'm no prophet, but I suspect that life was meant to contain more purpose and logic than the experience of a turtle on its back. We won't find out what that purpose is if we just lay down and die. Shoot, even the turtle will try to roll back over.

If God wants me to get hit by a Peterbilt, that's His business. In the meantime, my job is to be so busy living that I'm as hard to hit as possible.

Going to church in a handbasket

No matter what religion you are, Catholic, Mormon, Jehovah's Witness, or Democrat, getting ready to go to church on Sunday morning is a lot like going to hell.

If you have kids, the Sabbath Day usually begins with demonic screeching, gnashing teeth, and muttered curses. That's because no kid in their right mind wants to go to church. Church is boring. It's full of hard benches, humorless people, and long periods of listening to things you don't give a rip about. All the crayons and baggies of Froot Loops in the world won't change that.

When I was a kid I couldn't see the attraction of being good if heaven was anything at all like church. It only takes about a third-grade education to ask yourself what's the point of being good on earth if the reward in heaven is church forever?

As a reformed Sabbath guerilla, I know what my kids are up to when they start plotting against going to church. They give me all the same reasons I used as a kid.

"Why do I have to go?" is a common adolescent refrain in our house. "It's not like God will hate me if I don't."

True. But then children aren't really capable of understanding the complexities of God and obeying commandments until they're old enough for the IRS to tax. You have to put obedience to them in terms they can understand. My favorite is, "Because if you don't go, I'll run over your bike with the car."

Kids have two methods of getting out of church. Both methods include lying, which is technically a sin, but they don't care and I don't blame them. I'd lie like a rug to get out of hell, too.

The first of the two methods is to feign an illness or an injury. Tomorrow morning, at least one kid in every family (three in orthodox LDS families) will piteously complain of ailments ranging from stomach cramps to bullet wounds. When this happens in my home, I point out all the miraculous healing in the New Testament as proof that church is just the ticket for a compound fracture. Religion may not be the perfect health plan but it's cheaper than the hospital.

The second ploy is to lose an article of apparel necessary to attend church. I once told my mother that I lost all eleven pairs of my underpants. She made me go anyway. I was so traumatized by this unnatural experience that I never tried it again. I mean what if the Millennium had started and I wasn't wearing any skivvies?

Shoes are good to lose. So are pants. Most Christian mothers won't make their kid go to church without pants because it reflects poorly on them as parents. They'll risk having their own kids hate their guts forever but can't stand the thought of being regarded as bad parents by people they only see once a week. Go figure.

If going to church wasn't a commandment, it would be pointless. By the time parents finally get their kids to church, they aren't feeling particularly charitable or Christlike. They're so livid that the thoughts going around inside their heads would make Hitler blanch.

If God really intended Sunday to be a day of rest, kids would come permanent press with shoes permanently attached to their feet—and church would only be about four minutes long.

Who's turn *is* it *to be* the *d*evil?

I can always tell when the Jehovah's Witnesses show up at my house. The dog has a major conniption.

Chance, my dog, isn't prejudiced, she's stupid. She thinks the J-dubs are the ward visiting teachers whom she genuinely doesn't like. This isn't her fault either. I've trained her to bark at anyone carrying a casserole.

The J-dubs never come to see me. It's my wife they're after. They've pegged me as a lost cause ever since I tried to discuss a pressing theological issue: namely are the Three Stooges going to heaven? Larry and Curly maybe, but no way Moe. Come on, the guy was a jerk.

Even though we're Mormons, my wife lets the J-dubs in our house. She reads their magazines and talks to them. Consequently they keep coming back. I don't mind because they're nice people if a bit on the dumb side.

Oh, they are too.

Look, anyone who'd actually go door-to-door looking for converts in an area where the predominant religion thinks they're blood kin to the devil has to be a little feebleminded. I know because I've done it.

In fact, the first time I ever ran into the J-dubs was in the mission field. Only there we called them Tee-jays, short for *"Testigos de Jehova."* We called their Bible the "Green Dragon" for an equally absurd reason which I don't remember and I'm glad.

As a young missionary, I was told to watch out for the Tee-jays because they'd poach my investigators. I spent lots of time memorizing tried-and-true anti-Tee-jay scriptures. I even learned to admire veteran elders who could "Bible bash" with the Tee-jays in fluent Spanish. In short, I was an idiot.

Everything changed one day when I answered a knock on the door of our rathole apartment in Nalgas de Vaca. There on the steps were two old lady Tee-jays, *Watchtowers* in hand. Talk about your irony. Here I'd traveled 5,000 miles to spend the flower of my youth serving a full-time mission, only to get tracted out by some part-time grandma Tee-jays. It was almost enough to make me swear off religion.

For their part, the Tee-jay ladies were scared spitless by my own appearance. It wasn't hard to tell that they hadn't expected the devil to answer the door. I quickly hit them with a board.

Just kidding. What I did was give them 250 pesos (.0895 U.S. cents) for a *Watchtower*. We talked—actually they talked while I pidgined and waved my arms. I even got a tentative smile before they left.

A few days later, I saw the grandma Tee-jays again in the train station. My companion was stunned when they actually waved at us. Heretofore the Tee-jays had always crossed the street to get away from us. A week after that, a Tee-jay stopped and picked us up in his truck when one of our bikes got a flat out in the middle of nowhere.

It wasn't a spiritual experience. I just finally realized that despite everything I'd been told, I actually had more in common with the evil Tee-jays than not: they were good, honest, hardworking people, if a bit on the stubborn side when it came to their version of God.

I lost the first of many testimonies back then. It was a hard thing. I mean what's the world coming to when you can't count on someone to be the devil?

Overcome by the Spirit

Whatever religion you belong to, whatever your personal relationship with God, there is one thing we all hold in spiritual common—falling asleep in church.

There are a lot of reasons for conking off in the middle of a church meeting, not the least of which is that a five-minute dose of any church meeting is almost boring enough to be regulated by the Food and Drug Administration.

I've attended services of other faiths, so I know that snoozing while worshipping isn't just a Mormon thing. I sat next to a guy in a Catholic mass once who actually snored, something which I previously believed to be the sole province of Mormon high priests. I've worshipped with Jews, Prods, J-dubs, and assorted other faiths. They've all got their snoozers.

The only faith I've ever seen which emphatically believes in NOT sleeping in church was a black evangelical service I attended in Georgia. These people know how to get down to Christ. You'd have to be deaf to fall asleep in one of their meetings. Great music.

Everyone knows the Sabbath is a day of rest. Sleeping in church is merely an orthodox approach to this commandment. The more spiritual you are, the faster and deeper you sleep. Atheists, excommunicated types, and New Agers like me, being spiritually dim, just get bored in church.

Falling asleep in the middle of an LDS church meeting, like the priesthood, is primarily a male function. The older you get and the more priesthood you've got, the quicker you're overcome by the Spirit. Some high priests are asleep before the end of the opening song. Still others will close their eyes for a prayer and never return. A few will even sleep right through their own talks.

A common jest in the Mormon church is that a greater degree of reverence could be had in our meetings if we would simply ordain all infants to the office of high priests. It's true. The average LDS church service sounds like a gang of howler monkeys trapped in a dumpster. Make these kids high priests and they'll sleep through church.

Only occasionally do you see women asleep in church. I don't know why. I suspect it's because of something only women (and sharks) can do. Anyone raised by

a woman and married to a woman knows that women sleep with their eyes open.

It's not just church that produces sleep. Plenty of Sabbath naps take place in the home. I passed the big four-oh last year. I know that there is no form of Sunday worship more restful than flopping down on the front room floor with the dog after a big meal and conking off until the home teachers come around and wake me up.

The trouble with this kind of Sabbath snoozing is that it leaves you with a doozy of a hangover. Invariably I wake up in my own drool (I hope), feeling like an animal research group darted me for closer study. The rest of the day is anything but a spiritual experience. You drag around like the undead, wishing you'd resisted the Spirit just a little bit more.

Sleeping in church is nothing to be ashamed of. It's proof that despite our religious differences, we're all one faith.

Dawn of the selfish dead

Although Mormons take genealogy pretty seriously, we're not the only religion to maintain close ties with people long dead. Some Asian and native cultures actually keep their dead ancestors in the house. Mormons could take a cue here. Think how easy genealogy would be if Great-great-grandpa Fobbin and all eight of his wives were stored in the basement right along with the wheat?

I'd probably take genealogy more seriously if I hadn't fallen victim at an early age to *Ensign* faith promoting stories wherein the spirits of centuries-dead people start badgering live people to do temple work so the dead people can get on with business in heaven.

If these stories are true, and if a thousand years on

earth is indeed little more than an afternoon in heaven, then does it occur to anyone other than me that these spirits are a bunch of inconsiderate, self-centered nags? I mean come on, they haven't been dead five minutes and already they're bugging us to do their genealogy. And we're the ones with the time constraints.

In the interest of becoming more serious about genealogy, I signed up for my ward family history class. Last month, we went on a Sunday School field trip over to the regional Family History Center. The instructor showed us how to look up our family trees on the computer.

"See how far back your family histories go," she told us.

For people like me, how far back isn't nearly as interesting as how far OUT. Did you know that George Custer didn't get his temple work done until 1980? There's no mention of Sitting Bull. Ulysses S. Grant's work was done in 1927, but there were too many Robert E. Lees to tell for sure about Grant's arch nemesis. Maybe losing a war means you have to wait longer. Hey, you don't know.

I found a lot of Edward Teaches, but none with the *nom de guerre* of a bloodthirsty pirate. I'm prurient enough to wonder what old Blackbeard would think of having his temple work done by people he would have pillaged had he been alive.

As a Mormon, I hold to the party line that genealogy is important. It's also a lot of hard work. I traced my own family back to sixteenth-century England, where I discovered that one of my ancestors had a buttock torn off by the king's dogs for stealing a leek from the royal garden.

Just kidding. The computer will only tell you if all the pieces of your ancestor are entered on the record under one name. Which brings up the most aggravating part of genealogy: namely name changes. You may be enormously proud of your family name, but odds are it used to be something else. Like maybe Dogwallop or Crambungee.

It seems every Kirby family in early England named their sons Edward or John. Then, to be trendy in an empty-headed serf sort of a way, they changed the spelling of the last name approximately 132 times in the same century. Kirby is also Kerby, Curby, Kirbi, Kurbie, Korbey and—in one incredible feat of originality by some illiterate drudge who spent too many days harrowing a field without his hat—Corkbee.

When I'm dead, I'm coming back to bug my great-great-grandchildren for some laughs. I'm going to find the busiest one and impress on him the idiot idea that Kirby was spelled with a Z in the late 20th Century.

Tell your great-grandkids to watch for it in the *Ensign*.

Robert kirby: avenging angel

For a voice of wailing is heard out of Zion.
JEREMIAH 9:19

In church, parents with young children come in two categories: those who inflict church on their kids, and those who loose their kids on church.

I'm not complaining. Children are essential to religion. Just last week, in fact, I had a near faith promoting experience regarding prayer and kids in church.

A baby across the aisle from me was screeching and carrying on while trying to ferret another Froot Loop out of her mother's purse. The parents seemed oblivious to the fact that their baby was making it hard for others to hear or sleep. Concerned about reverence in the chapel, I said a little prayer, asking for the Lord's help in maintaining reverence. Darned if it didn't work.

The child lost its balance and fell, conking its fuzzy noggin on the back of a pew. It took another full minute for La Tiffany VerDawnette's parents to realize that she wasn't going to stop wailing like an Iraqi air raid siren. Only then did they finally drag her out into the foyer where she wouldn't disturb the meeting.

OK, I'm not saying that the Lord pushed the kid off the pew. He probably had an angel do it. If so, I doubt it was because of my prayer. After all, "Will someone please shut that little milk sucker up?" isn't exactly formatted as a prayer. I'll bet someone more righteous than me said a real prayer. Maybe the bishop.

Reaction from the orthodox to this very un-*Ensign*, near faith promoting experience is probably shock, maybe even rage among Nazi Mormons. My response to that is that it's sometimes easier to thump a kid on the gourd than it is to make the parents more considerate of others. I won't swear that this is an eternal truth, but then you can't prove that it isn't, either.

None of this is a complaint about kids. It's more a complaint about inconsiderate parents. Truth is, noisy kids can be very handy in church. Especially if you want to get out of church yourself.

When my daughters were young, I used to secretly torment them during opening exercises. By the time the practice song was over, they were starting to cry. Smiling self-consciously, my wife and I would take our weeping brood out into the foyer. Twenty minutes later, we're

BROTHER KIRBY—THE PORTER ROCKWELL OF REVERENCE

dragging our boat down to the lake so our kids wouldn't bother anyone.

Some people bribe their kids to keep them quiet in church. Others threaten their children. In my ward, you can guarantee your kids will be quiet if you promise them a Nintendo or threaten to make them sit next to Brother Kirby.

When you're six years old, sitting next to Brother Kirby is not a good thing. That's because Brother Kirby is the Orrin Porter Rockwell of reverence. I dislike noisy kids almost as much as I hate boring fast and testimony meetings. I stay awake in one by mounting secret campaigns of terror against the other.

I consider it a major success if a kid near me breaks out into shrieks during the meeting. It's easy if I borrow a thumbtack from the ward bulletin board. Harder if my only options are evil looks and whispered threats.

OK, it's cruel and heathen to torment pew monkeys in church, but I've noticed that on Super Bowl Sundays, all the fathers want to sit their kids next to me.

"Dear, LeNephi has a tack stuck in his forehead. I'll have to take him out to the car and calm him down by listening to the radio."

All of this leaves a lasting impression of reverence on kids. Half of our Primary now becomes incontinent on the eve of the Super Bowl. My own kids are almost grown now, but they still whimper when they water ski.

Perfect *is* as perfect does

My wife and I have never been able to resolve a fundamental religious question. It's the sort of question that can lead to a holy war if not handled with reverence and sensitivity. The question: What does God look like?

After years of careful study and thought, I say God looks like a harried Burl Ives. Hey, you can't prove He doesn't.

Irene says there's no way God looks like Burl, mainly because Burl is bald and fat. Whatever God looks like, she says, it would have to be perfect and Burl isn't perfect. Rubbish. When you're the Creator of the universe, perfect is what YOU say it is.

When it comes to what God looks like, all Christians have to go on is the widely interpreted scripture that God made us in His image. That and the description of assorted angels. Personally, I don't find the appearance of angels all that comforting because orthodox Christianity holds with cherubs and wings and harps and other weird stuff. If true, heaven is going to be full of a bunch of chubby albino bats.

The only reason it even matters what God looks like is the resurrection. If we're really created in God's image, and we're all going to get our bodies back after death, what are we going to look like? It's an important gospel question.

Because we're Mormons and believe in eternal marriage, Irene says, "I hope perfect is Alec Baldwin. What's the point of the resurrection if your spouse is going to look like a beanbag chair?"

Herein lies the quandary: perfection. Namely, whose version. If it's God's version (and it probably is), perfection very well could mean that all you hard bodies out there are going to look like Aunt Bee for eternity. On the other hand, if perfection means that we get the kind of bodies WE think are perfect, then we're all in a lot of trouble.

The one thing people have shown God down here is that when it comes to how we look, we have this astounding penchant for going to the extreme. Silicon, collagen, dyes, hormones, steroids, there's nothing we won't take, shoot, implant, or daub on in order to make ourselves more "perfect."

It's even worse when it comes to our clothes. I'll bet it drives God crazy to see us down here blowing serious money on fashions—money that could otherwise be used to help the poor. Most people in America spend more time thinking about their jeans than they do the homeless.

If God let us have our way in the resurrection, there's no telling where we'd end up. Heaven would be full of women trying to one-up Cher, walking around with lips that looked like catcher's mitts and bazooms that arrived ten minutes before the rest of them. Men would be buff to the point of looking like dump trucks.

God will probably handle the resurrection the way He handles everything else—meaning we'll get what's best for us. Judging from the sorts of things that have happened to me already as a Christian, I don't find this exactly comforting because it'll invariably be something designed to keep me meek and humble.

Get ready to look like Burl Ives.